WELCOME
TO HANUKKA...

We love latkes as much as the next person, but TBH, reciting the same blessings for eight nights in a row (if you actually remember or are home to do them) doesn't exactly inspire Joyous Judaism. JewBelong to the rescue! We have two Hanukkah skits! (Bet you didn't even know you needed one!) The first is about some badass Maccabees and a talking pig named Seymour, and the other is about a little-known wonder woman, Judith, whose superpower is getting a bad dude drunk and chopping his head off. In addition to the traditional candle blessings (in Hebrew and in English to avoid JewBarrassment), we have short candle-lighting readings for each night highlighting Jewish/universal values that will help us all be better people, plus songs, jokes, and more.

Happy Hanukkah!

Love, **team jewbelong**

TABLE OF CONTENTS.

■ CONTEMPORARY CANDLELIGHTING

Hanukkah is a heartwarming opportunity for reflection and inspiration. Combining candle lighting with these readings will make your Hanukkah celebration even more meaningful. Some of them are specifically Jewish, but more are based on the universal values we all hold in our hearts. Try it this way: read about peace the first night and then add acceptance the second night and so on. By the eighth night, you will have a lot of wisdom!

PEACE The first Hanukkah candle of the year sparks a call for peace. Just as the world wasn't peaceful in the time of the Maccabees, it's still not peaceful today. **"When the power of love overcomes the love of power, the world will know peace."** Let this candle be a spark for peace for me, my family and friends, and everyone on the earth. **–JIMI HENDRIX**

ACCEPTANCE The second Hanukkah candle sparks acceptance. Gaining acceptance of ourselves and others relieves aggravation and makes room for love. On this night, let's remember that **"Most people need acceptance a lot more than they need advice."** **-BOB GOFF**

REPAIRING THE WORLD The third Hanukkah candle sparks a desire to repair the world. There is so much to do, but what if each of us really considered it our responsibility? **"There once was a man who stood before God, his heart breaking from the pain and injustice in the world. 'Dear God,' he cried out, 'look at all the suffering and the anguish in your world! Why don't you send help?' God replied, 'I did. I sent you.'"** **-RABBI DAVID WOLPE**

THE GOLDEN RULE The fourth Hanukkah candle sparks treating people how we would want to be treated. Someone once asked the wise Rabbi Hillel to stand on one foot and quickly teach him the entire Torah! So, Rabbi Hillel stood on one foot and said, **"That which is hateful to you, don't do to anyone else. All the rest is commentary."** Sometimes people call this the "Golden Rule." Whatever you want to call it, let's let the fourth candle remind us to treat others as we would want to be treated. **-RABBI HILLEL**

COMPASSION The fifth Hanukkah candle sparks compassion; compassion for ourselves, our friends, animals, even those we don't like that much. Being compassionate can change everything. **"You can either practice being right or practice being kind." -ANNE LAMOTT**

DIVERSITY The sixth candle sparks the importance of honoring how diverse our world is. **"No one is born hating another person because of the color of his skin or his background or his religion [or sexual orientation]. People must learn to hate, and if they can learn to hate they can learn to love, because love comes more naturally to the human heart." -NELSON MANDELA**

FORGIVENESS Forgiveness is not just for Yom Kippur. The seventh candle sparks forgiveness, which in some cases is wildly difficult to achieve but is always worth the effort. **"The first to apologize is the bravest. The first to forgive is the strongest. The first to forget is the happiest." -UNKNOWN**

GRATITUDE We are at the end of Hanukkah – the big finale! The final eighth candle sparks gratitude. **"Showing gratitude is one of the simplest yet most powerful things humans can do for each other."** **-RANDY PAUSCH**

TRADITIONALLY, ON THE FIRST NIGHT of Hanukkah, you read blessings #1, #2 and #3. And then, for the next seven nights, you just read #1 and #2. However, #3, the Shehecheyanu, is such a sweet prayer about gratitude that we like to include it on all eight nights.

Now, before you jump right in, you need to put the candles into the menorah. And, yes, there is a tradition for this. You are supposed to place the candles in the menorah from right to left, and then light them left to right. After an exhaustive Google and rabbi search, we still don't know why. By the way, the wax in Hanukkah candles almost always drips, so put foil or something under the menorah to protect your table.

You will notice that your menorah has one taller candle holder than the others. This is for the shamash, or "helper" candle. On the first night of the holiday, put candles in the shamash and the far-right candle space. On the second night, you will need three candles. One for the shamash, the far-right candle space, and the one next to it. And then every night, you add one more candle, until on the last night you have filled up all the spaces on the menorah. For those who are not math whizzes, this means you need 44 candles for the whole holiday. Unless you have more than one menorah. Then you're on your own. Oh, Hanukkah candles are thin and sometimes break, so get extra.

When you are ready to start, light the shamash candle with a match. Then take the shamash and use it to light the other candles, left to right. And then, put the shamash back in its spot and recite the blessings!

According to tradition, you are supposed to place the menorah near your front window, facing the street, because lighting them is bringing light into the world that could frankly use more light. Also, it is a beautiful idea to show your neighborhood the light that comes from inside your home. In addition, it can be a beautiful sign of a multicultural community. But be careful if you have curtains. Or racists in the neighborhood. Also, don't blow the candles out unless you are really running late and worried about missing the beginning of the movie. Then there is probably some rabbinic exception. But seriously, you are supposed to let them burn out on their own. Add a little interest by making bets on which candles will burn out first and last.

Place the candles
RIGHT TO LEFT

Light the candles
LEFT TO RIGHT

BLESSING OVER THE **HANUKKAH CANDLES**

Baruch atah Adonai, Eloheinu melech ha-olam,
asher kidshanu bemitzvotav vitzivanu lehadlik neir shel Hanukkah.

Praised are You, God, Spirit of the Universe,
who makes us holy through your commandments
and commands us to light the Hanukkah candles.

BLESSING FOR **HANUKKAH**

Baruch atah, Adonai Eloheinu melech ha-olam,
she'asah nisim la'avoteinu, bayamim haheim baziman hazeh.

Praised are you, God, Spirit of the Universe,
who performed miracles for our ancestors in their day at this season.

SHEHECHEYANU: **GENERIC PRAYER OF GRATITUDE**

The Shehecheyanu is a great generic catchall prayer that's basically saying,
"Wow! We are really happy we got to this moment!" Like for example, after the JewBelong
website goes live and doesn't crash after working our asses off for months to make it
perfect, we will say Shehecheyanu.

Baruch atah, Adonai Eloheinu melech ha-olam,
shehecheyanu v'key'manu v'higiyanu lazman hazeh.

Praised are You, God, Spirit of the Universe,
who keeps us alive, sustains us, and brings us to this moment.

HANUKKAH OH HANUKKAH
Rabbi Rami M. Shapiro

Hanukkah, Oh, Hanukkah
Come light the menorah
Let's have a party
We'll all dance the hora
Gather 'round the table, we'll give you a treat
A dreidal to play with and latkes to eat
And while we are playing
The candles are burning low
One for each night, they shed a sweet light
To remind us of days long ago
One for each night, they shed a sweet light
To remind us of days long ago

BLESSING FOR ANYONE WHO ISN'T JEWISH
('Cause we know this is a lot)
Inspired by Rabbi Janet Marder

May everyone who shares in a Jewish life feel welcome and integrated. We lovingly acknowledge the diversity of our community and are deeply grateful for the love and support you provide by opening your heart to Judaism, no matter how big or small a part it is in your day. Your presence at this Jewish experience is valued. It is not taken for granted because not everyone in this broken world will sit at a Shabbat dinner or attend a Passover Seder. We are a very small people and history has made us smaller. As we once again see a rise in hatred and hear fear in the voices of our community, we are grateful for your presence. We pray with all our hearts that all you give to the Jewish people will come back to you and fill your life with joy. Amen.

Add when reading to a family raising kids:

We offer special thanks to those who are raising their sons and daughters with Jewish identity. Our children mean hope, life and future. With all our hearts, we want to thank you for your love and willingness in giving the ultimate gift to the Jewish people. Amen.

A JEWBELONG PROMISE TO WORK TOGETHER TO END ANTISEMITISM

Antisemitism is on the rise and we must all do our parts to stop it. Jews and allies need to be courageous, to call it out and to never make excuses for it. Antisemitism isn't new, but there are new and insidious strains of it. There's the familiar white supremacy movement that pretty much hates everyone who doesn't look like them, the run-of-the-mill antisemites, the subtle I-don't-really-mean-it -when-I-talk-crap-about Jews kind, and a relatively new form of hate directed at Israel which crosses the line to antisemitism far too often. Antisemitism is hate. Jews, Christians, Muslims, Hindus, atheists... literally everyone is worse off for it. Are we going to end it completely? Probably not. But that doesn't give us permission to throw our hands up and accept it, make excuses, or discount it. It's exactly the opposite. We must talk about it, write about it, learn about it, and call it out. No matter how difficult or uncomfortable, we can't ignore, chuckle along, or accept it. We've already learned the bitter lesson that true hate is never little, it is never unimportant, and it should never, ever be ignored.

DREIDEL SONG
(Like Rudolph the Red-Nosed Reindeer, this is an old favorite from every second grade Holiday concert. Ever.)
Samuel S. Grossman + Samuel E. Goldfarb

I have a little dreidel
I made it out of clay
And when it's dry and ready
Then, dreidel I shall play

CHORUS: Oh, dreidel, dreidel, dreidel
I made it out of clay
And when it's dry and ready
Then, dreidel I will play

It has a lovely body
With legs so short and thin
And when it gets all tired
It drops and I will win

CHORUS: Oh, dreidel, dreidel, dreidel
I made it out of clay
And when it's dry and ready
Then, dreidel I will play

My dreidel is so playful
It loves to dance and spin
A happy game of dreidel
Come play now, let's begin

CHORUS: Oh, dreidel, dreidel, dreidel
I made it out of clay
And when it's dry and ready
Then, dreidel I will play

■ SO, DREIDEL, DREIDEL, DREIDEL...

For the life of us, we don't get the whole dreidel thing. It may be the dullest game ever. It started when the ancient Jews were hiding in caves learning Torah. They would play dreidel for a break. Some break! We'd almost rather study Torah. But we don't want to sound too much like Scrooge, (oops, wrong holiday) so here's more about dreidel. Each side of the dreidel bears a letter of the Hebrew alphabet, which together form the acronym for Nes Gadol Hayah Sham — "A great miracle happened there." Fun fact: In Israel, dreidels feature the acronym for "A great miracle happened here."

Here's how you play:

Each player begins with an equal number of game pieces (M&Ms, gelt, quarters, or whatever you think will help make the game a little more exciting). We recommend starting with 10-15 game pieces each. (TBH, we have a feeling that you won't want this game to go on for too long.)

To start the game, every player puts one game piece into the center. Then everyone takes a turn spinning the dreidel. The player with the highest spin (nun is highest, followed by gimmel, then hey and finally shin) goes first. If you get a tie for first, everyone spins again.
Now the "fun" begins...

The first player spins the dreidel. When it stops:

If ‫נ‬ (nun) is facing up, the player does nothing.

If ‫ג‬ (gimmel) is facing up, the player gets everything in the pot.

If ‫ה‬ (hey) is facing up, the player gets half of the pieces in the pot. If there's an odd number, we say don't be greedy or try to split the game piece – just leave it in the pot for the next winner.

If ‫ש‬ (shin) is facing up, the player adds one of their game pieces to the pot.

Then the next player goes, and you keep taking turns. Once a player runs out of pieces, they are "out" or they can ask another player for a "loan." (We'd be shocked if someone actually wanted to keep playing by asking for a "loan" but there's a first time for everything.) When one player has won all of the pieces, it's game over. Yay!

For the love of God, if you know a way to make Dreidel a more exciting game, let us know. Lots of people play for gelt, which is German for money, but for the purposes of Hanukkah, it's those chocolate coins wrapped in gold or silver foil that come in a nifty mesh bag. (Depending on the brand, the chocolate may or may not be worth the trouble of getting those foil covers off.)

ROCK OF AGES
Ma'oz Tzur

Rock of Ages let our song
Praise thy saving power
Thou amidst the raging foes
Was our sheltering tower.
Furious, they assailed us,
But thine armour veiled us.
And thy word broke their
sword When our own strength
failed us. And thy word broke
their sword When our own
strength failed us.

Hebrew: *Maoz tzur y'shuati*
l'cha naeh l'shabeach
Tikon beit t'filati
v'sham todah n'zabeach.
L'eit tachin matbeach
mitzar hamnabeach
Az egmor b'shir mizmor
chanukat hamizbeach
Az egmor b'shir mizmor
chanukat hamizbeach.

▌ JOKES

TWO MENORAHS
Two menorahs are sitting in the window.
The first one says, "Wow, it's getting hot with all these candles."
The second one says, "Woah, a talking menorah!"

GIFT LISTS
Q: What's the best Hanukkah gift for someone who has everything?
A: A burglar alarm.

HANUKKAH MANNERS
It was just before Hanukkah and Miriam, a grandmother, was giving directions to her grown up grandson who was coming to visit with his wife for the first time since Miriam had moved to her new apartment.

"You come to the front door of the condominium complex. I am in apartment 3A." Miriam told her grandson.

"There's a big panel at the door. Use your elbow to push button 3A and I will buzz you in. Come inside and the elevator is on your right. Get in the elevator and use your elbow to press the 3 button. When you get out, my apartment is on the left. Use your elbow to ring my doorbell and I'll open the door for you."

"Grandma, that sounds easy," her grandson replied, "But why am I hitting all these buttons with my elbow?"

Miriam answered, "You're coming to visit empty handed?"

■ THE OILY MIRACLE OF HANUKKAH

DIRECTOR'S NOTE:
You can either read this skit free-form by going around the table and having everyone take turns, or you can assign parts, or you can just have two people take turns reading... whatever makes your Hanukkah kick-ass! If you're going big, then you'll want to include the following props: A jug (empty milk gallon works fine), a mop, a bucket and cleaning supplies, and a plastic sword. Have fun!

CAST OF CHARACTERS:
MACCABEE 1 (17 lines)
WIFE 1 (15 lines)
MACCABEE 2 (12 lines)
WIFE 2 (12 lines)
SEYMOUR (A PIG) (9 lines)
NARRATOR (7 lines)

> *Casting should be done completely blind of all gender, age, and/or classic "beauty" bias, to avoid any level of prejudice.
>
> Raw talent, on the other hand, should be considered.

NARRATOR: The setting is the Second Temple in Jerusalem, 160 B.C.E. The Maccabees have just retaken Judea after defeating the mighty armies of Antiochus IV.

MACCABEE 1: Well, we did it! We Maccabees beat back the evil Antiochus! We stood up to his gigantic armies, and poof! They were gone.

WIFE 1: "Poof?" It took eight years.

MACCABEE 1: Don't start with me. I've been at war. I'm tired. I'm hungry. And my sciatica is acting up something fierce.

MACCABEE 2: I'm just glad we can finally get back into the Temple. Praying in a dirty tent all these years has been just awful. Let me just get this door open. (CREEKY NOISE. OPENS DOOR TO TEMPLE.) Oy vey!

WIFE 2: What is it? Did the Greeks put up those tacky Zeus statues of theirs? Or the one of that homewrecker Aphrodite?

MACCABEE 2: No, this is much worse! Look!

EVERYONE: OH NO!

WIFE 1: This looks like that time we left the kids alone for the weekend!

MACCABEE 1: They ruined our temple! The benches are broken! The walls are cracked! And look, is that a red wine stain on the carpet? That's never going to come out.

WIFE 2: What a pig-sty!

SEYMOUR: I beg your pardon?

[ALL FOUR HUMANS SCREAM.]

MACCABEE 1: It's a pig! A pig can't be here in our temple! Pigs aren't kosher!

WIFE 1: The pig is talking! And you're worried that he's not kosher?!

WIFE 2: It's a demon! Quick, slay him with your sword.

NARRATOR: The Maccabees wield their swords and lunge toward Seymour.

SEYMOUR: I'm pretty sure that's not necessary.

MACCABEE 2: Stop talking! You're not supposed to talk, pig!

SEYMOUR: Actually, the name's "Seymour." And so what if I'm not supposed to talk? I'm not supposed to be lying on the altar of a Jewish temple, either. But the Greeks brought me here to sacrifice me.

WIFE 1: So why are you still alive?

SEYMOUR: How do I know? I'm a pig. But I assume they ran out of time before fleeing Judea. In any case, here I am, alive and well.

MACCABEE 1: Well, I'm very glad they didn't kill you...

WIFE 1: You're making friends with a pig now?

MACCABEE 1: Quiet, I'm having a conversation here. So listen, pig... uh, Seymour... we just really need you to leave now.

SEYMOUR: That's fine, I'm going. Now that the Greeks have left, and you guys are back in charge, I don't have to fear for my life. I mean, it's not like any of you are going to eat me. Oh, and one more thing – you're almost out of oil. Ta ta. (HE EXITS.)

MACCABEE 2: I sure hope that pig was wrong about the oil. Because we've got to keep the eternal light burning at all times to show our devotion to God. Every temple has one.

WIFE 2: Let me check the storage room. There's usually plenty of oil in there.

NARRATOR: Wife 2 goes into the storage room and comes out holding a small oil jug.

WIFE 2: The pig didn't lie. This is it... just enough to keep the fire lit for about a day.

WIFE 1: That will never be enough! The eternal light will go out! This is just terrible!!

MACCABEE 1: Can't we just make more oil?

WIFE 2: Excuse me? Do you know how long it takes to make oil? Eight days.

MACCABEE 1 & MACCABEE 2: (IN UNISON.) Eight days?!

WIFE 1: What, you think olives grow on trees?

MACCABEE 1: Don't they?

WIFE 1: Well, yeah, but first you have to pick the olives, and then you have to press them, and then the oil needs to sit before it will keep a flame burning. It's an eight-day process. What can I tell you?

MACCABEE 2: What are we going to do?

WIFE 2: Don't fret too much. You've been at war for eight years. You can't start worrying about olive oil.

WIFE 1: That's right. Let's go home and try to get some sleep. At least we have enough oil for the flames to burn through the night and tomorrow we can come back and clean up this mess.

ALL EXCEPT WIFE 1: OK.

NARRATOR: The next morning they all come back to the temple with mops and buckets.

MACCABEE 1: I'm not looking forward to this. I can't remember the last time I had to clean up such a mess.

WIFE 1: Yeah, that's because you've never cleaned a thing in your life. Look... the eternal light. It's still burning!

MACCABEE 2: That's weird. It's been over eight hours since we were here. Shouldn't the oil have burned out by now?

WIFE 2: Hey, don't look a gift horse in the mouth.

SEYMOUR: (POPPING HIS HEAD UP FROM BEHIND THE ALTAR.) I'm not a horse. I'm a pig.

MACCABEE 1: Seymour! What are you doing back here?

SEYMOUR: It was so cold out last night, and I could see through the windows that the flame was still burning, and it looked kind of cozy, so I figured I'd bunk down here.

MACCABEE 1: Well, you've got to go. And for good this time!

SEYMOUR: (EXITING.) Yeah, I'm going, I'm going.

WIFE 1: That's some persistent pig. All right, I'll start on the floors. You all take the walls and the benches.

NARRATOR: Four days later, at sunset everyone is still cleaning the temple.

MACCABEE 2: I don't get it. It's been five nights, and that eternal light is still burning.

MACCABEE 1: You sure you didn't add any oil to it?

WIFE 1: And where would I get this oil from? I told you it takes eight days. So it'll be three more days before we have any new oil. That's basic math, genius.

WIFE 2: What if the eternal light is... haunted?

MACCABEE 2: We just had a talking pig in here, and you're scared of an eternal light?

WIFE 2: Well, how is it doing this? How is the oil not running out? Is it magic? Is it a spell? Is it a curse?

(LOUD BOOM SOUND!!!!)

WIFE 1: Well, I think we just got our answer.

MACCABEE 1: This isn't magic. And it's not haunted. It's God. God is keeping the oil burning for us until we can make more of it. It's a miracle!

MACCABEE 2: So if he can keep the oil burning for eight nights, why can't he clean up this mess himself?

WIFE 2: Because we can do that ourselves. What we can't do is keep one night's worth of oil burning for eight nights.

MACCABEE 2: Well, it's only been five nights. Talk to me three days from now, and then I'll tell you whether it's a miracle or not.

NARRATOR: Three days later everyone comes back to the temple.

MACCABEE 2: You were right! It is a miracle!

WIFE 2: See? I told you.

MACCABEE 1: God kept the oil burning for eight nights, just like he led us to victory over the Greeks. And he let us clean up this temple and make it holy again.

MACCABEE 2: You know what we should do? Let's have a big celebration tonight... and then every year at this time we'll celebrate for eight nights!

WIFE 1: Yes! And I'll make potato latkes and jelly donuts with the extra oil! And we can eat chocolate coins and not worry if we gain a few pounds!

SEYMOUR: (PEAKS BEHIND THE TEMPLE DOOR.) Sounds great! Am I invited?

ALL IN UNISON: EVERYONE'S INVITED! HAPPY HANUKKAH!

▌JUDITH AND THE SALTY CHEESE

DIRECTOR'S NOTE:

You can either read this skit free-form by going around the table and having everyone take turns, or you can assign parts, or you can just have two people take turns reading... whatever makes your Hanukkah kick-ass! If you're going big, then you'll want to include the following props: Salty cheese, a bottle of wine (Manischewitz is best), a wine glass and a plastic sword. Have fun!

CAST OF CHARACTERS:

MACCABEE 1 (19 lines)

BAKER (19 lines)

JUDITH (A BEAUTIFUL JEWISH WIDOW) (10 lines)

JUDITH'S MAID (7 lines)

HOLOFERNES (AN ASSYRIAN GENERAL) (9 lines)

NARRATOR (8 lines)

> *Casting should be done completely blind of all gender, age, and/or classic "beauty" bias, to avoid any level of prejudice.*
>
> *Raw talent, on the other hand, should be considered.*

NARRATOR: The setting is a battle during the Maccabee uprising against the Assyrian occupation of Judea, circa 168 B.C.E. Scene 1 takes place in the town of Bethulia, near Jerusalem.

MACCABEE: Hey there. I'm a Maccabee.

BAKER: Oh, wow. That's my favorite cookie. Kind of a specialty of mine!

MACCABEE: No – not a macaroon – a Maccabee. Anyway, I'm here to tell you a cool Hanukkah story you may never have heard before – the story of Judith and the Salty Cheese.

BAKER: I'd rather hear a story about macaroons.

MACCABEE: Shush. You'll like this story. So, around 168 B.C.E...

BAKER: Whoah – "B.C.E.?" What is that, some sort of boy band?

MACCABEE: No – it means "Before the Common Era." Just think of it as the year 3593, because that's what it was on the Jewish calendar. Anyway, during this time, the Jews were fighting to retake the land of Judea after it had been invaded by the Assyrians.

BAKER: The Syrians invaded our land?

MACCABEE: Not the Syrians – the Assyrians.

BAKER: What's an Assyrian?

MACCABEE: The Assyrians lived in what is now northern Iraq, which used to be ruled by the Greeks.

BAKER: This is getting very confusing. Were we fighting the Assyrians, the Iraqis, or the Greeks?

MACCABEE: That's not important right now! The point is, it was a seriously tough battle. There were only a few hundred Maccabees fighting thousands of Assyrians. And to make matters worse, the Assyrians had the meanest, toughest general we ever saw. His name was Holofernes.

BAKER: His name was what?

MACCABEE: Holofernes!

BAKER: That's like the worst name ever. It sounds like a potted plant. Maybe that's why he was so mean?

MACCABEE: Maybe. Anyway, his mission was to defeat the Jews. And it was working, too. Holofernes had cut off their food and water supply, and they were quickly running out of everything.

BAKER: Even macaroons?

MACCABEE: ENOUGH WITH THE MACAROONS! THERE ARE NO MACAROONS IN THIS STORY!

BAKER: Oh, OK. Sorry.

MACCABEE: All right, I'll add some macaroons at the end if you'll just let me get through this part.

BAKER: Deal.

MACCABEE: OK. Luckily for us, there was a beautiful Jewish woman named Judith. She was a widow who was tired of seeing her people oppressed by the Assyrians. So she hatched a plan.

JUDITH: I have hatched a plan! I shall go to see Holofernes, along with some salty cheese, a bottle of wine, and my trusty maid.

MAID: I'm the maid.

BAKER: Wait – why does Judith have a maid?

MACCABEE: Everyone had a maid in those days.

BAKER: But I mean like, if her people were oppressed and didn't even have enough food and water, how did she have wine and cheese? And for that matter, how could she afford a maid?

MAID: Excellent question.

MACCABEE: Quiet! Judith, I'm sorry. Please continue.

JUDITH: Thank you. I shall go with this salty cheese, some wine, and my trusty maid

[SHOOTS BAKER A LOOK.] who continues to work for me even though I can't pay her right now. I may wind up dead, but I've got to try to save my people. But first, I need to put on some foxy clothes. Maid, fetch me that red backless Valentino and the black Manolo slingbacks.

MAID: These are her clothes. And yet she can't afford to pay me.

NARRATOR: Judith and Maid exit.

BAKER: Wait – why is Judith putting on foxy clothes to take on an evil general? How is that going to... oh, I see where this is going.

NARRATOR: Judith and the Maid enter the Assyrian camp.

JUDITH: Yooo hooo... Holofernes!

HOLOFERNES: Who dares enter my camp? I shall smite you and make you rue the day you... **[SPOTTING JUDITH.]**... whoah. Well, hello. You're mighty foxy. Who are you?

JUDITH: Hi, I'm Judith. And you're mighty handsome yourself... for an evil general who wants to starve my people to death, that is.

HOLOFERNES: Wow! Thanks! How about if you hang out here while I figure out how I'm going to kill every last one of those Jewish Maccabees?

JUDITH: That sounds perfect. But you know what? You look a little tired and hungry. Why don't you come to my tent and rest while my maid whips you up a little snack?

HOLOFERNES: Your maid? **[SPOTS MAID.]** Oh, hey. I didn't even notice you were here.

MAID: Story of my life.

HOLOFERNES: OK, well, I guess I could use a nosh.

NARRATOR: Holofernes and Judith go into his tent.

JUDITH: Maid, give the general some of my delicious cheese.

MAID: Yes, your majesty.

NARRATOR: Maid hands Holofernes a big piece of white cheese.

HOLOFERNES: Wow. This is delicious. Hey, this cheese is making me so thirsty.

JUDITH: Maid, give the general some of my delicious red wine.

HOLOFERNES: Oh, I really shouldn't drink before going into battle.

JUDITH: Oh, don't worry. I'm sure your army is going to be victorious. They've got you to lead them, and you're such a big, strong hunk of a man.

MAID: I gotta admit, she's pretty good at this.

HOLOFERNES: I guess you're right. All right, pour me some of that wine. **[MAKES GULPING SOUNDS.]** Woooh – that's really sweet. But it goes down well with the salty cheese.

NARRATOR: Maid pours him another glass of wine, which he guzzles down as he eats another big chunk of cheese.

HOLOFERNES: Yeah, that's delicious. **[HICCUP.]** Oh, man. I'm getting really sleepy.

JUDITH: Then why don't you just lie down for a minute?

HOLOFERNES: Well... all right – just for a little while. Don't let me sleep more than 45 minutes, OK? Cuz I really gotta go kill some Jewzzzzzzzzz...

NARRATOR: Holofernes falls asleep and begins to snore loudly. Judith then grabs his sword from his belt.

JUDITH: Sweet dreams, sleepyhead. And speaking of your head... HA-YA!

NARRATOR: Judith wields the sword and chops Holofernes's head off.

MAID: HOLY CRAP! YOU JUST CHOPPED HIS HEAD OFF! I did NOT see that coming!

BAKER: Me neither! This story is crazy!

MACCABEE: And you won't believe what happened next. Judith took Holofernes's head and hung it outside the tent for all the Assyrians to see. Once they saw their general had been slaughtered, and by a woman, they completely freaked out! And the Maccabees got a second wind when they saw what a champ Judith was, and they kicked some Assyrian ass!

BAKER: And THEN they all ate macaroons?

MACCABEE: [SIGHS.] Yeah, then they all ate macaroons to celebrate. And because of Judith and her incredible bravery, in addition to the latkes and jelly donuts that we eat on Hanukkah, we also eat salty cheese.

BAKER: Like Feta?

MACCABEE: Sure, like Feta.

BAKER: I have another question.

MACCABEE: Of course you do.

BAKER: Actually, two. Why do we spell "Hanukkah" so many different ways, and why is it that we remember the Maccabees, who were super-fit and strong like you, by eating heavy fried food and cheese?

MACCABEE: Those, my friend, are very good questions that even I can't answer. Now I'm really hungry, so when I count to three, all listeners and actors wish each other Happy Hanukkah with feeling! One... two... three!

ALL IN UNISON: HAPPY HANUKKAH!

A JEWBELONG
SHABBAT SUPPLEMENT!

Since there are eight days of Hanukkah and only seven days in the week, simple calendar math will tell you that there is at least one day of Hanukkah that falls on a Friday night, so it's basically a doubleheader Shabbat/Hanukkah extravaganza! Also, truth be told...JewBelong Shabbat is the BEST and it would be a shame if you missed it for an entire year. Like last year.

▌REFLECTION

Take a minute to remember what you were doing last Friday night when Shabbat started. Yes, this is the point where you feel the urge to go run for your phone and check your calendar, 'cause who can remember what they were doing last Friday night? When you have it, or at least an idea, use it as a starting point to think about the past week. Think about its ups and downs and about the regular parts of this past week too. And then... Let it go. When we clear our head and heart of the hustle of the week then we can truly rest. This rest is magic because it helps us bring our best selves to the week ahead.

Where was I last Shabbat? Where was I physically and spiritually? Was I rushed, or did I savor the coming of Shabbat? What's happened in the six days past? They go so quickly that I have hardly taken notice. What kind of person was I this week? Thoughtful? Superficial? Preoccupied? Appreciative? Did I laugh? Cry? Did I tell anyone how much I love them? Did I use my week well? And what does that even mean? What lessons will I take with me into the future?

As I enter into Shabbat, I release the past week – its joys and its sorrows. I free myself from any misgivings or guilt. I am ready to look for new happiness and bring the best of me to new experiences during the week to come.

■ "THE RESET" AKA "SHABBAT"

According to tradition, Shabbat is not simply a good idea, but a Mitzvah. The Ten Commandments say: "Remember Shabbat, and set it apart. Six days you shall toil and do all your work, but the seventh day is the day of rest." In 11th century France, the medieval sage, Rashi, focused on a curious part of the commandment: "Six days shall you toil and do all your work. How, he asked, can you complete all your work in six days?"

Rashi understood what we still face today: That there is simply more work to get done each week than we can possibly manage. Said Rashi, "When Shabbat comes, it should seem to you as if all your work is completed, even though it isn't. You should stop thinking about work." Friday evening is designed to help us perform this magic trick, to begin to act as if our work is done.

The concept of a day of rest was also alien to many ancient people. The Greeks and Romans ridiculed this peculiar tradition, accusing ancient Jews of laziness for resting one day out of every seven. But while Shabbat is called a day of rest, it would be a mistake to think of it as a lazy day because real rest is restorative. It recharges us spiritually, as well as physically. Our transition from work to rest can begin as early as Thursday, which was market day. Preparation of the Shabbat meal began, and we wished each other "Shabbat Shalom." Shabbat can free us to spend time with those we love, to savor small moments that usually pass unnoticed, freeing us to reflect on what matters most. The candles, readings, songs, and wine are all here to help set the mood, creating an atmosphere of warmth.

DAY OF REST
Sung to the tune of "Be Our Guest" From Disney's Beauty and the Beast
Lyrics by Adam Sank

Day of rest, day of rest
Fridays really are the best
Light the candles, say the blessings,
Let your spirit do the rest

Glass of wine, challah bread,
Or a dinner roll instead
We don't care if you're not Jewish
Black, white, purple, pink or bluish

Take a break, from the week
Rest your head and weary feet
'Cuz Friday nights are never second-best
Invite your friends to dine,
Serve them a lot of wine,
Day of rest, day of rest, day of rest!

Day of rest, day of rest
Put our Shabbos to the test
Paper plates or fancy dishes
Try the tsimis – it's delicious

Tell some jokes, sing some songs,
On Shabbat, you can't go wrong
Spend some time at your own table
Bake a kugel if you're able

Throw your cares, to the wind
Let tranquility begin
This weekly holiday is heaven-blessed
So come and lift your glass,
Another week has passed

Day of rest, day of rest, day of rest!

BLESSINGS FOR CHILDREN

Parents and children, stand near one another. Parents put their hands on their child's head and then recite the blessing out loud.

▌TRADITIONAL CHILDREN'S BLESSING

(FOR SONS) May God make you like Ephraim and Menasheh.
(FOR DAUGHTERS) May God make you like Sarah, Rebecca, Rachel and Leah.
(FOR SONS AND DAUGHTERS) May God bless you and protect you. May God's presence shine on you and be good to you. May God reach out to you tenderly and give you peace.

▌FOR EVERY STEP ALONG THE ROAD...
Adapted from Mah Tovu's Rabbi Ken Chasen and Rabbi Yoshi Zweiback

Here with you beside me, I feel so greatly blessed.
This moment means much more than I can say.
A time to be together, a time for us to rest.
Shabbat is here.
The time has come to celebrate the day.
So I hold you close, my hands upon your head.
As I watch you growing, I smile through my tears;
Sometimes I wish you'd stay forever small.
But then I see you blossom, and I befriend the passing years.
I love you now, I'll love you then, I love to see it all.
So I lift my voice to offer you this prayer,
for every step along the road, I will be there.

▌WISHES FOR MY CHILD

Our dependent and delicious newborn,
Our self-assured and adventurous youngsters,
Our rebellious yet loving teenagers...
As our children keep changing,
Growing from infancy to adulthood,
Our relationship with them keeps changing too.
But our wishes for them stay the same always.
We want them to be blessed with health and happiness;
We want them to know how much they are loved.

While in our hearts, we wish the very best
for our children every moment of every day;
We want to take this time each week to bless our children
as it encourages us to express our wishes for them out loud.
May I have the wisdom to know what blessing my child truly needs.
May my child be able to receive my blessings
and to know my love is deep and unconditional.

PRAYER FOR COUPLES
A JewBelong Original

There is an ancient blessing, Eishet Chayil, generally translated as A Woman of Valor that is recited in many observant Jewish homes on Shabbat. The husband recites the blessing to give honor to his wife. Sweet, right? During the blessing he compares her to rubies and compliments the cleanliness of the house, and how well she sews curtains and bakes bread. While JewBelong is all for blessing or declaring love for one another as much as possible, Eishet Chayil may not resonate the way it did back in the shtetl. JewBelong's modern version is an alternative way for all couples to show appreciation to one another. Enjoy!

(PARTNER 1)
To you, my partner, I say: "Thank you."
Thank you for being you, in all your flawed perfection
Thank you for sharing your heart and your life with me
For your laughter and your tears
Your strength and your struggles
Your certainty and your doubts
Thank you for growing with me and not away from me
For talking and for listening
For arguing and for making up
For seeing and being a light in the darkness
For all these things, I say: "Thank you."

(PARTNER 2)
To you, my partner, I ask: "Please."
Please see me as I am, in all my flawed perfection.
Please show me compassion and understanding
Through my breakdowns and breakthroughs
My triumphs and tribulations
My miracles and meltdowns
Please continue growing with me and not away from me
Seeing the goodness in my soul
The sincerity of my love
And my desire to continue building this life with you
For all these things, I ask: "Please."

(BOTH PARTNERS IN UNISON)
To you, I say: "Thank you."
To you, I ask: "Please."
To you, I pledge my love
And with God's blessing, may we enjoy the best of times together. Amen.

LIGHTING SHABBAT CANDLES

We light two candles for the two commandments related to Shabbat – Observe and Remember. We circle our hands across the top of the candles three times, washing the light toward ourselves, and then cover our eyes as we recite the blessing. We close our eyes before the prayer, and when we open our eyes at the end of the blessing, we have entered into Shabbat.

בָּרוּךְ אַתָּה ה׳ אֱלֹהֵינוּ מֶלֶךְ הָעוֹלָם אֲשֶׁר קִדְּשָׁנוּ בְּמִצְוֹתָיו וְצִוָּנוּ לְהַדְלִיק נֵר שֶׁל שַׁבָּת. אָמֵן.

Baruch atah, Adonai Eloheinu melech ha-olam, asher kid'shanu b'mitzvotav v'tzivanu lihadlik ner, shel Shabbat. Amen.

We praise God, Spirit of Everything, who has made us holy with your Mitzvot and commanded us to light the Shabbat light. Amen.

HA-MOTZI

Traditionally, this blessing is made over a Challah, a traditional sweet braided bread. If you don't have a Challah, use any other bread, cracker, pizza crust, or whatever you like:

בָּרוּךְ אַתָּה ה׳ אֱלֹהֵינוּ מֶלֶךְ הָעוֹלָם הַמּוֹצִיא לֶחֶם מִן הָאָרֶץ. אָמֵן.

Baruch atah, Adonai Eloheinu melech ha-olam ha'motzi lechem min ha'aretz. Amen.

Blessed are you, Lord our God, Spirit of the Universe Who brings forth bread from the earth. Amen.

KIDDUSH
BLESSING OVER THE WINE

בָּרוּךְ אַתָּה ה׳ אֱלֹהֵינוּ מֶלֶךְ הָעוֹלָם בּוֹרֵא פְּרִי הַגָּפֶן.

בָּרוּךְ אַתָּה הי אֱלֹהֵינוּ מֶלֶךְ הָעוֹלָם אֲשֶׁר קִדְּשָׁנוּ בְּמִצְוֹתָיו וְרָצָה בָנוּ וְשַׁבַּת קָדְשׁוֹ בְּאַהֲבָה וּבְרָצוֹן הִנְחִילָנוּ זִכָּרוֹן לְמַעֲשֵׂה בְרֵאשִׁית. כִּי הוּא יוֹם תְּחִלָּה לְמִקְרָאֵי קֹדֶשׁ זֵכֶר לִיצִיאַת מִצְרָיִם. כִּי בָנוּ בָחַרְתָּ וְאוֹתָנוּ קִדַּשְׁתָּ מִכָּל הָעַמִּים וְשַׁבַּת קָדְשְׁךָ בְּאַהֲבָה וּבְרָצוֹן הִנְחַלְתָּנוּ בָּרוּךְ אַתָּה ה׳ מְקַדֵּשׁ הַשַּׁבָּת. אָמֵן.

Baruch atah, Adonai Eloheinu, Melech ha-olam, asher kid'shanu b'mitzvotav v'ratzah vanu, v'Shabbat kodsho, b'ahavah uv'ratzon hinchilanu, zikaron l'ma'aseh v'reishit. Ki hu yom t'chila, l'mikra'ei kodesh, zecher l'tziat Mitzrayim. Ki vanu vacharta, v'otanu kidashta, mikol ha'Amim. V'Shabbat kodshecha b'ahavah uv'ratzon hinchaltanu. Baruch atah, Adonai, m'kadeish haShabbat. Amen.

And there was evening and there was morning, the sixth day. The heavens and the earth were finished. And on the seventh day, God ended all the work and rested. And God blessed the seventh day.

We praise God, Spirit of Everything, creator of the fruit of the vine. Amen.

Blessed are You, who sanctifies us with commandments and has been pleased with us. You have lovingly and willingly given us Your holy Shabbat as an inheritance in memory of creation. The Shabbat is the first among our holy days and remembrance of our exodus from Egypt. Indeed, You have chosen us and willingly and lovingly given us Your holy Shabbat for an inheritance. Blessed are You, who sanctifies the Shabbat. Amen.

▌A SHABBAT REQUEST

Help us to feel peaceful this new Shabbat.
After noise, we seek quiet;
After crowds of indifferent strangers,
We seek to touch those we love
After concentration on work and responsibility,
we seek freedom to listen to our inward selves.
We open our eyes to the hidden beauties
and the infinite possibilities in the world;
We break open the gates of goodness and
kindness in ourselves and in others.

NOTES:

Made in United States
Troutdale, OR
11/30/2024

25561775R00017